2022
Washington, D.C.

Restaurants

The Food Enthusiast's
Long Weekend Guide

Andrew Delaplaine

Andrew Delaplaine is the Food Enthusiast.
When he's not playing tennis,
he dines anonymously
at the Publisher's (considerable) expense.

James Cubby – Senior Editor

The Food Enthusiast's Long Weekend Guide

Table of Contents

INTRODUCTION

Because it is our nation's Capital where so much of our history is remembered in national institutions such as the Smithsonian. If you can't feel like an American here, you're not trying. Walking the Mall or staring up at Lincoln's grim visage sitting in his marble chair. He walked the same path you are walking. It's a very sobering experience to visit the

Capital, and something every American should do at least once.

Besides all the marble monuments, imposing edifices and traffic congestion, there's fabulous shopping, lots of free museums, great restaurants, a nightlife scene as active as most other places and vibrantly humming communities living the life of Washington every day and every night.

Politics is to Washington what movies are to L.A., so whatever bar you find yourself in after a long day traipsing through museums, be careful: you might be standing next to a White House assistant or a CIA spy. You never know what will happen in Washington.

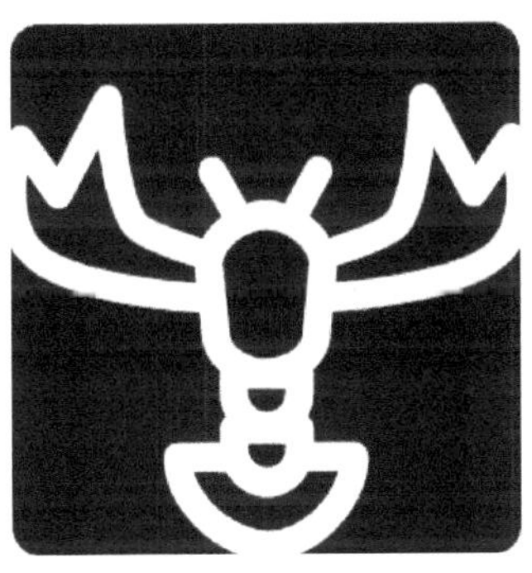

MOUNTAIN OF DESPAIR,
STONE OF HOPE

GETTING AROUND

BY CAR

But only if you must. They have gone out of their way to make brining a car downtown one of the worst hassles anywhere in the country. There are speed traps, red light cameras, almost no parking, unannounced street closings, you name it. If you drive here, plan on parking your car and leaving it while you make use of the increasingly user-friend mass transit options. **Personally, I use UBER and LYFT.**

WALKING

No kidding. This is one of the best towns for walking I can think of. Since they've made parking such a hassle downtown, and the public transportation has gotten so good, many people leave their cars at home.

When you use pubic transport to get downtown, you'll find yourself walking a lot anyway because so many of the capital's attractions are strung along the Mall, so the easiest way to get to them is by walking.

The Metro system is good, and with trains, buses and even bikes in common use, getting around is easier than you think.

The Transportation Department has a web site explaining all the options. It's very clear-cut. GoDCgo - www.godcgo.com/

METRO

The Metro is DC's subway system. It's pretty good. It has 5 color-coded lines that are easy to use. Numerous station are downtown where the system runs underground.

METROBUS

A little more complicated for the visitor, but very useful if you can figure out the routes.

CIRCULATOR BUS

dccirculator.com/

The DC bus system used to be pretty bad, but the circulator Buses are great and very tourist-friendly. They also go places hard to reach by the Metro.

They are like shuttles in the sense that they run on a fairly predictable schedule (every 10 minutes or so) and go between main attractions and the city's most popular neighborhoods for visitors. Costs $1. All D.C. Circulator routes run every ten minutes and cost $1. There are currently five routes.

TAXI
There are hundreds of taxis circulating if you're in a hurry.

The A to Z Listings
Ridiculously Extravagant
Sensible Alternatives
Quality Bargain Spots

AGORA
1527 17th St. NW, Washington, DC: 202-332-6767
www.agoradc.net
CUISINE: Mediterranean, Greek, Turkish
DRINKS: Full bar
SERVING: Dinner
PRICE RANGE: $$
Another neighborhood spot with a popular happy hour. Besides the typical Mediterranean fare they serve small places like Brussels Sprouts, Zucchini pancakes and Duck Salad, all worth ordering. Good choice for Brunch if you like this type of food. Outdoor patio for warm weather.

THE ARSENAL AT BLUEJACKET
300 Tingey St SE, Washington, DC, 202-524-4862
www.bluejacketdc.com
CUISINE: Traditional American

DRINKS: Full bar
SERVING: Lunch & Dinner – daily; Sunday Brunch; Closed for lunch on Mon
PRICE RANGE: $$
NEIGHBORHOOD: Navy Yard
Some come to this industrial chic eatery for the great selection of beers and ales and others come for the eats and a good time. Menu offers creative American favorites such as: Pierogi, Wurst Sandwich and Meatball Stroganoff. Popular date spot. Seating inside and out – weather permitting.

B TOO
1324 14th St. NW, Washington, DC, 202-627-2800
www.btoo.com
CUISINE: Belgian
DRINKS: Full Bar
SERVING: Lunch, Dinner

PRICE RANGE: $$$
NEIGHBORHOOD: Logan Circle
This beautiful restaurant, showcasing Belgian cuisine and culture, has two levels with an open kitchen. Look for owner Bart Vandaele, who competed on "Top Chef." Great place for brunch as the menu features nice different types of waffles. Dessert waffles include a vanilla waffle with ice cream and chocolate sauce.

for Brunch. Dining room is Beaux Arts design with 30-foot ceilings, period chandeliers and turn of the century elegance. Great service and friendly staff. Top-notch American favorites like Fried Chicken, Pineapple Ham and Catfish Fingers.

BAD SAINT

3226 11th St NW, Washington, No Phone
www.badsaintdc.com
CUISINE: Filipino
DRINKS: Full bar
SERVING: Dinner
PRICE RANGE: $$$
NEIGHBORHOOD: Columbia Heights
Cozy (very intimate—only a couple of dozen seats)
upscale Filipino eatery with a rotating menu. Even
though the lights seem very bright at night, they are
high above you, so the atmosphere is disarmingly
intimate. Favorites: Goat braised in lemongrass;
Chicken liver mousse; and Purple radishes.
Vegetarian options. Creative cocktails. Reservations
necessary – booked **months** in advance. (However,
I've sometimes lucked into a seat when I walked in,
even though I had to wait a bit.)

BAR PILAR

1833 14th St. NW, Washington, DC: 202-265-1751
www.barpilar.com
CUISINE: American, Bar
DRINKS: Full bar
SERVING: Brunch, Lunch, Dinner
PRICE RANGE: $$
Popular two-level bar with Euro-chic ambience. Great brunches but best for late night snacks like tapas and entrees like Roasted Beet Salad and Mussels. Friendly crowd.

BARRACKS ROW

731 8th St SE, Washington, DC, 202-544-3188
www.barracksrow.org
For the past decade, Barracks Row Main Street has worked tirelessly to preserve and enhance Capitol Hill's historic 8th Street, SE, commercial corridor and to revitalize its business community. The group's focus is the five blocks of 8th Street that stretch south from Pennsylvania Ave S.E. to the terminus of 8th Street at the Washington Navy Yard along M Street, S.E. Barracks Row is located eight blocks east of the U.S. Capitol.

BANANA CAFÉ & PIANO BAR

 500 8th Street, SE, Washington, DC, 202-543-5906 ·
www.bananacafedc.com
CUISINE: Cuban, Puerto Rican, Tex Mex
DRINKS: Full Bar
SERVING: Lunch, Dinner
PRICE RANGE: $$

NEIGHBORHOOD: Capitol Hill/Barracks Row
Tasty food and friendly staff. Great beef burritos.
Outdoor patio and upstairs piano bar.

BEEFSTEAK

800 22nd St. NW, Washington, DC, 202-296-1439
www.beefsteakveggies.com
CUISINE: Fast Food/Vegetarian
DRINKS: No Booze
SERVING: Lunch & Dinner
PRICE RANGE: $$
NEIGHBORHOOD: Foggy Bottom
This healthy eatery from José Andrés' restaurant
group offers a creative menu of veggie & grain bowls.
Salads and vegetables – that's what you'll get here.
When he says beefsteak, he means "beefsteak
tomato." As the chef puts it, "A tomato, an asparagus
or a broccoli is just as powerful as a cow or a
chicken." I couldn't **disagree** with him more.

BELGA CAFÉ

514 8th St. SE, Washington, DC: 202-544-0100
www.belgacafe.com
CUISINE: Belgium
DRINKS: Full bar
SERVING: Lunch, Dinner, Brunch
PRICE RANGE: $$
The original Belgian restaurant in DC. Great
authentic Belgian food and Belgian Beers. Features
an open kitchen, European casual dining room along
with a sidewalk cafe.

BEN'S CHILI BOWL
1213 U St NW Washington, DC, 202-667-0909
www.benschilibowl.com
CUISINE: Hot Dogs, American (Traditional)
DRINKS: No Booze
SERVING: Breakfast, Lunch & Dinner; closed for
Breakfast Sun

PRICE RANGE: $
NEIGHBORHOOD: U Street Corridor
This iconic spot has been around forever and everyone from Martin Luther King Jr to President Obama has eaten here. The menu is simple but a great place to stop for a late night snack. The most popular item here is the "Half Smoke" – a half beef & half pork sausage on a bun, topped with mustard, chopped onions and chili. The second most popular is the decadent Chili cheese fries. Cash only.

BIRCH & BARLEY
1337 14th St. NW, Washington, DC, 202-567-2576
www.birchandbarley.com
CUISINE: American
DRINKS: Full Bar
SERVING: Breakfast, Lunch, Dinner

PRICE RANGE: $$$
NEIGHBORHOOD: Logan Circle
Comfortable neighborhood type restaurant serving
eclectic fare and an impressive collection of 500
artisan beers (in the upstairs **ChurchKey Bar**).
Delicious menu items like: fried chicken served with
donuts; ruffled herbed mac & cheese; and fig &
prosciutto flatbread.

THE BOMBAY CLUB

815 Connecticut Ave. NW, Washington DC: 202-
659-3727
www.bombayclubdc.com
CUISINE: Indian
DRINKS: Full bar
SERVING: Lunch, Dinner, Brunch
PRICE RANGE: $$$
The Bombay Club emulates characteristics of the old
clubs of India serving gourmet Indian cuisine serving
four types of Indian cuisine: Parsi Fare, Goan
Specialties, Moghlai Specialties, and Coastal Cuisine.
Delicious food, good service. Live piano.

BUSBOYS AND POETS
2021 14th St. NW, Washington, DC: 202-387-7638
www.busboysandpoets.com
CUISINE: American
DRINKS: Full bar
SERVING: Breakfast, Brunch
PRICE RANGE: $$
Bookstore and café. A local hangout. Menu includes
everything from Fallafel to chicken wings and garlic
mashers. Great ambiance and excellent service.
Reasonable prices.

BUA THAI CUISINE RESTAURANT & BAR
1635 P St. NW, Washington, DC: 202-265-0828
https://buadc.com/
CUISINE: Thai
DRINKS: Full bar
SERVING: Lunch, Dinner
PRICE RANGE: $$
Dupont Circle Thai Restaurant with a friendly
welcoming atmosphere. Food is almost always good
and reasonable. Favorites include: Guong Pad Tang
(duck curry) and Gai Ta Kite (grilled pepper
chicken). Good service. Try the upstairs deck if
weather permits. Great happy hour specials.

CAFÉ 8
424 8th Street, SE, Washington, DC, 202-547-
1555 ·
https://www.thecafe8.com/
CUISINE: Mediterranean
DRINKS: Full Bar

SERVING: Lunch, Dinner
PRICE RANGE: $$
NEIGHBORHOOD: Capitol Hill/Barracks Row
Casual dining with friendly service. Great
Turkish food and pizzas. Outdoor dining.

CAFE BERLIN

322 Massachusetts Ave. NE, Washington, DC: 202-
543-7656
www.cafeberlin-dc.com
CUISINE: German
DRINKS: Full bar
SERVING: Lunch, Dinner
PRICE RANGE: $$
Located in Capital Hill, this German eatery is a
locals' favorite. Typical German fare with dishes like
Wiener Schnitzel, gooseberry pie and German beer.
Outdoor seating.

CAFÉ MILANO

3251 Prospect St. NW, Washington DC: 202-333-6183

www.cafemilano.net

CUISINE: Italian

DRINKS: Full bar

SERVING: Lunch, Dinner

PRICE RANGE: $$$

This high-end Italian eatery is a favorite of local celebrities, athletes and politicians. If you don't mind "the scene" you'll enjoy the sophisticated atmosphere, great food and excellent service. Wine cellar.

CAFÉ SAINT-EX

1847 14th St. NW, Washington, DC: 202-265-7839

https://cafesaint-ex.com/

CUISINE: American

DRINKS: Full bar

SERVING: Lunch, Brunch, Dinner

PRICE RANGE: $$

Here you'll find a cozy pub atmosphere with bar, small dining
area and an outdoor patio. Standard farc with a twist like Roast Chicken, laced with pistachio butter, and Rib-Eye Steak, served with sweet-potato fries. Grilled Tuna also receives raves here. Two levels of seating. Dine early as this place gets packed after 9 p.m.

CAVA MEZZE

527 8th Street, SE, Washington, DC, 202-543-9090

www.cavamezze.com

CUISINE: Greek, Mediterranean

DRINKS: Full Bar
SERVING: Lunch, Dinner
PRICE RANGE: $$
NEIGHBORHOOD: Capitol Hill/Barracks Row
Authentic Greek mezze "small plates". Menu favorites include: Crazy feta, Haloumi Sliders, and Saganaki. Indoor and patio dining (in season).

CHIPOTLE MEXICAN GRILL

601 F St. NW, Washington, DC, 202-347-4701
www.chipotle.com
CUISINE: Mexican
DRINKS: No Booze
SERVING: Lunch
PRICE RANGE: $
NEIGHBORHOOD: Georgetown
Mexican fast food fare. Great burritos and tasty tacos. Always fresh and reportedly the best location of the chain. Several D.C. locations.

COMMISSARY

1443 P St. NW, Washington, DC: 202-299-0018
www.commissarydc.com
CUISINE: American
DRINKS: Full bar
SERVING: Breakfast, Lunch, Dinner
PRICE RANGE: $$
Located in Logan's Circle. Comfortable and casual atmosphere. Sofas, lots of TVs and free WiFi. Great breakfast and popular happy hour. Menu features everything from authentic tacos (hard to find in DC), breakfast quesadillas, chicken nachos and vegetarian options.

Trelissed garden at The Dabney

DABNEY
122 Blagden Aly NW, Washington, 202-450-1015
www.thedabney.com
CUISINE: American (New)
DRINKS: Full bar
SERVING: Dinner
PRICE RANGE: $$$
NEIGHBORHOOD: Shaw, Downtown
Set in a former row house, this rustic eatery offers a
menu of Mid-Atlantic cuisine, sourced from the very
finest purveyors, farmers and fishermen in the area.
They get great use out of the wood-burning hearth—

some of the food is cooked just the way they did it 200 years ago. You can see everything going on in the open kitchen. Menu picks: Sorghum-glazed short rib and Catfish sliders. Many of the dishes are meant to share. Has a few seats outdoors.

DEL MAR

791 Wharf St SW, Washington, 202-525-1402
www.delmardc.com
CUISINE: Spanish / Seafood
DRINKS: Full bar
SERVING: Lunch, Dinner
PRICE RANGE: $$$
NEIGHBORHOOD: Southwest DC
Spanish villa-like eatery offers an upscale dining experience. The chef's other restaurants are Italian,

but this one focuses on Spanish coastal cuisine, so lots of flavorful seafood dishes. (His business partner was born in Spain.) Chef is a James Beard winner & also Michelin-starred. As stuffy as all that sounds, the mood here is just the opposite—lively, fun, busy. Favorites: Calamari paella and Basque tapas. Nice wine selection – amazing sangria. Waterfront views.

DUPONT ITALIAN KITCHEN
1637 17th St. NW, Washington, DC: 202-328-3222
www.dupontitaliankitchen.com
CUISINE: Italian, Pizza
DRINKS: Full bar
SERVING: Lunch, Dinner, Brunch
PRICE RANGE: $$
This place has a big gay following but a locals' favorite. Indoor and outdoor seating. Food is good and service is excellent (most of the time). Big portions. Great pizza and tiramisu to die for.

EL SAPO CUBAN SOCIAL CLUB
8455 Fenton St, Silver Spring, MD, 301-326-1063
www.elsaporestaurant.com
CUISINE: Cuban
DRINKS: Full Bar
SERVING: Dinner
PRICE RANGE: $$
Out of the Beltway over in Silver Spring is this
modern eatery serving classic Cuban fare. Being from
Miami, I know the real thing when I see it. Or eat it,
that is. This place is bright, colorful, fun and busy.
Favorites: Ropa Vieja (a beef dish that means 'old
clothes,' don't ask me why) and Berro, Field Greens
& No Oil salad. Happy hour specials. Nice homestyle
Cuban desserts.

EL TAMARINDO

1785 Florida Ave NW, Washington, DC, 202-328-3660

<u>www.eltamarindodc.com</u>

CUISINE: Salvadoran / Mexican

DRINKS: Full Bar

SERVING: Lunch, Dinner

PRICE RANGE: $$

Popular late-night eatery (though it's open all day) with a creative menu of Salvadoran and Mexican cuisine. I recommend ordering the Salvadoran dishes over the Mexican—you can get Mexican food anywhere in the country, but not Salvadoran cuisine. This place has been around since the early 1980s. They've thrown everything from somebody's attic onto each inch of wall space in the little restaurant, and even from the ceiling you'll find flags handing down, posters everywhere, little pieces of bric-a-brac. Very busy on the eye. But colorful, very colorful. I'd say nothing they've put on the wall since they opened has even been taken down. My Favorites: Beef cmpanadas and Revuelta (pork & cheese) pupusas. If you didn't know already, a pupusa is a robust cake or flatbread cooked on a griddle and made from cornmeal or rice, usually cornmeal. Into this humble piece of bread they stuff various ingredients, basically whatever you have in the house. But in a restaurant you have choices, from cheese to pork rinds to refried beans to squash or whatever. Authentic places serve cole slaw with a pupusa, but it's a spicier cole slaw than we see in the U.S. In El Salvador, they eat

pupusas with their hands, not forks, and you can too.
This place offers complimentary chips and salsa.

ESTADIO
1520 14th St. NW, Washington, DC, 202-319-1404
www.estadio-dc.com
CUISINE: Spanish, Tapas
DRINKS: Full Bar
SERVING: Lunch, Dinner
PRICE RANGE: $$$
NEIGHBORHOOD: Logan Circle
Friendly restaurant with an open kitchen so you can
see the food being prepared. Great tapas. Chef Haidar
Karoumi's menu favorites include: roasted sweet-
corn salad and a bocadilllo—a small sandwich on
home-baked bread with crispy pork belly and pickled
shishito pepper. Impressive wine list with more than
400 wines, most from Spain.

FIREFLY
1310 New Hampshire Ave. NW, Washington, DC:
202-861-1310
www.firefly-dc.com

CUISINE: American, Organic, Gluten-free
DRINKS: Full bar
SERVING: Brunch, Lunch, Dinner
PRICE RANGE: $$
Neighborhood restaurant in downtown DC near Dupont Circle featuring local, organic menu and American comfort food. Great a la carte brunch from a gluten free menu that included cheesy grits, bacon and fruit cup. Great service. Sandwiches, salads, entrees.

FLORIDA AVENUE GRILL
1100 Florida Ave NW, Washington, DC, 202-265-1586

www.floridaavenuegrill.com
CUISINE: Diner/Soul Food
DRINKS: No Booze
SERVING: Breakfast, Lunch & Dinner
PRICE RANGE: $$
NEIGHBORHOOD: U Street Corridor
Open since 1944, local greasy spoon serves up simple menu of diner fare and down-home Southern classics. This place has lots of character and so does the food. Dishes like Fried catfish over grits with 2 sunny side up eggs – delicious. Other Southern favorites like Pan fried chicken and Smothered pork chops.

FOUNDING FARMERS

1924 Pennsylvania Ave NW, Washington, DC, 202-822-8783
www.wearefoundingfarmers.com
CUISINE: American Traditional
DRINKS: Full bar
SERVING: Breakfast, Lunch & Dinner
PRICE RANGE: $$
NEIGHBORHOOD: Foggy Bottom
Co-op owned American eatery with a menu of creative comfort food that's enjoyed with the same gusto by suited lobbyists as well as blue collar workers. Menu favorites include: Spicy Ahi Tuna Poke and Glazed Cedar Plank Salmon. Great place for breakfast—the beignets are made to order. Try the red velvet pancakes with cinnamon syrup and whipped cream cheese butter. Your arteries will not thank you, but your stomach will.

FOX & HOUNDS LOUNGE

1533 17th St. NW, Washington, DC: 202-232-6307
www.foxandhoundslounge.com/
CUISINE: American
DRINKS: Full bar
SERVING: Dinner, Breakfast, Brunch
PRICE RANGE: $

A good hangout with reasonable prices. Outdoor seating, perfect for people watching on a warm night. Good selection of nosh food like the Crab Cake Sandwich, Portobello Sandwich and Chicken Tenders. Also entrees like Lobster Dinner. Drinkers rejoice at the heavy pours.

GEORGIA BROWN'S

950 15th St. NW, Washington, DC: 202-393-4499
www.gbrowns.com
CUISINE: Southern

DRINKS: Full bar
SERVING: Brunch, Lunch, Dinner

PRICE RANGE: $$$
If you're a fan of Southern cuisine then this is the place. You'll find dishes like: Fried Green Tomatoes, Charleston Perlau, Louisiana Devil Shrimp and Southern Fried Chicken. Don't forget to order a Mint Julep. Live jazz on Wednesday nights. Great service.

HANK'S OYSTER BAR
1624 Q St NW, Washington, DC, 202-462-4265
633 Pennsylvania Ave SE, Washington, DC, 202-733-1971
www.hanksoysterbar.com
CUISINE: Seafood
DRINKS: Full bar

SERVING: Lunch & Dinner
PRICE RANGE: $$
NEIGHBORHOOD: Dupont Circle
Like a spot you'd find in New England, this bar offers up a great selection of seafood, clams, lobster rolls, raw bar, Chesapeake Bay rockfish (which happens to be Maryland's official state fish—who knew?) with a rotating list of daily specials. They even have their own oyster specially cultivated for this restaurant— the **Hayden's Reef**, an oyster they worked to develop with Dragon Creek Aqua Farm. Make sure you try a side order of the Old Bay Fries, lightly covered with the unique Maryland spice mix. Great happy hour deals. Main dining room, outdoor seating and three bar areas.

JALEO
480 7th St NW Washington, DC, 202-628-7949
www.jaleo.com/dc

CUISINE: Spanish, Tapas
DRINKS: Full Bar
SERVING: Lunch, Dinner
PRICE RANGE: $$$
NEIGHBORHOOD: Penn Quarter
This ever-popular eatery is the flagship enterprise of the world-famous Chef Jose Andres. Yes, folks, it all grew from this joint. Well, it's not quite a 'joint.' It's sleek, modern, stylish, and not as pricey as you might expect for a Jose Andres eatery. Here they serve his traditional Spanish fare like tapas, paella and sangria. Everything, of course, is expertly prepared because Jose Andres is nothing if not picky. Favorites: Salpicón de cangrejo (jumbo lump crab, cucumbers, peppers, tomatoes, cauliflower & a hefty dose of brandy sauce) and Tortilla de patatas al momento (Spanish omelette, potatoes, onions). Delicious Spanish desserts. I'd recommend reserving ahead.

JAVA HOUSE DC
1645 Q St., NW, Washington, DC: 202-387-6622
www.javahousedc.net
CUISINE: Coffee, Tea
DRINKS: No Alcohol
SERVING: Coffee, snacks.
PRICE RANGE: $$$
It's all about the location here, the best thing about Java House. Excellent coffee – beans roasted on premises, fresh bagels, poor service.

KRAMERBOOKS & AFTERWORDS CAFÉ
1517 Connecticut Ave. NW, Washington, DC: 202-387-1400
www.kramers.com
CUISINE: Café fare
DRINKS: Full bar
SERVING: Breakfast, Sunday Brunch, lunch, desserts
PRICE RANGE: $$
Bookstore with café open since 1976. First Bookstore/Café in the country to feature cappuccino, espresso, a full bar and food. An institution with locals. Live music Wed. – Sat.

LA TOMATE
1701 Connecticut Ave. NW, Washington DC: 202-667-5505
www.latomatebistro.com
CUISINE: Italian
DRINKS: Full bar
SERVING: Lunch, Dinner, Brunch
PRICE RANGE: $$
A friendly neighborhood bistro that serves affordable regional Italian cuisine. Great views on the patio. New Prosciutto Bar. Quality service and excellent food.

LAOS IN TOWN

250 K St NE, Washington, DC, 202-864-6620
www.laosintown.com
CUISINE: Laotian / Vegan
DRINKS: Full Bar
SERVING: Lunch, Dinner
PRICE RANGE: $$
This is a popular eatery offering classic Laotian cuisine. There's a separate menu for hard-core vegans. The interior here is modern, clean, sharp-edged. There's plenty of outdoor seating and I'd sit out there if the weather permits. Favorites: Grilled beef and Khua mee (which is a dish of sweet fried noodles). Interesting desserts like Khao Niao (that's a hot mango pudding).

LAURIOL PLAZA

1835 18th St. NW, Washington, DC: 202-387-0035
www.lauriolplaza.com

CUISINE: Latin American, Spanish, Tex-Mex
DRINKS: Full bar
SERVING: Lunch, Dinner
PRICE RANGE: $$
Great Mexican fare and delicious margaritas (Voted
Best Margaritas by Washington City Magazine –
2011). Try the Pechuga De Pollo, the Derango Platter
and the sangriarita – the perfect combination of a
margarita and sangria. Huge restaurant with dining
room and upstairs patio. Excellent service.

LAVAGNA
539 8th St SE, Washington, DC, 202-546-5006
www.lavagnadc.com
CUISINE: Italian
DRINKS: Full Bar

SERVING: Lunch, Dinner
PRICE RANGE: $$
NEIGHBORHOOD: Capitol Hill/Barracks Row
Fresh Italian fare in a friendly atmosphere. Popular
spot for Sunday brunch with lots of specials and
menu favorites like Goat and Pepper Preserve Omelet
with unlimited mimosas.

LE DIPLOMATE
1601 14th St NW Washington, DC, 202-332-3333
www.lediplomatedc.com
CUISINE: French café
DRINKS: Full Bar
SERVING: Breakfast, Lunch, Dinner, Brunch
PRICE RANGE: $$$
NEIGHBORHOOD: Logan Circle
A celebration of the French café serving everything
from the classic Onion Soup Gratinee to Steak Frites

and Escargots. Delicious desserts. Tasty crusty
baguettes made in-house. Reservations recommended.

LITTLE SEROW
1511 17th St NW, Washington, DC, 202-332-9200
www.littleserow.com
CUISINE: Thai
DRINKS: Beer & Wine Only
SERVING: Dinner
PRICE RANGE: $$$
NEIGHBORHOOD: Dupont Circle
A great Thai-inspired restaurant run by Chef Johnny
Monis that consistently gets rave reviews. (His other
restaurant, **KOMI**, is Greek, like Johnny.) The chef
will send out to your table 6 or 7 dishes to be served
family-style. Menu favorites include Khao tang gapi
(salted prawn/cilantro/peanut with fried rice cake) and
Ma hor (sour fruit and dried shrimp served with palm
sugar).

LOGAN TAVERN
1423 P St. NW, Washington, DC: 202-332-3710
www.logantavern.com
CUISINE: Bar, Burgers, American
DRINKS: Full bar
SERVING: Lunch, Dinner, Brunch
PRICE RANGE: $$
Local tavern with friendly crowd. Great place for
brunch. Good food, good service. Popular spot for
dinner. Dinner menu

selections include: Ginger Calamari - Flash Fried, Buffalo Shrimp with Spicy Blue Cheese Sauce, Portabella & Eggplant Sandwich with Feta Cheese and Sun-Dried Tomato Pesto, and 'Big Texas' Grilled Burger & Slow Roasted BBQ Brisket with Cheddar & Red Onions.

LOLA'S BARRACKS BAR AND GRILL
711 8th St SE, Washington, DC, 202-547-5652
www.lolasdc.com/
CUISINE: American
DRINKS: Full Bar
SERVING: Lunch, Dinner, Late Night
PRICE RANGE: $$
NEIGHBORHOOD: Capitol Hill/Barracks Row
This comfortable grill with a pub-like atmosphere offers a great place for a quick lunch or dinner. Menu favorites include: Chicken salad sandwich, sliders, and fish tacos. Friendly service.

MAKETTO

1351 H St NE, Washington, 202-838-9972
www.maketto1351.com
CUISINE: Cambodian / Taiwanese
DRINKS: Full bar
SERVING: Breakfast, Lunch, Dinner
PRICE RANGE: $$
NEIGHBORHOOD: H Street Corridor
Popular modern creative spot that combines 3 things
and does it very well in my opinion: a marketplace
featuring a restaurant and coffee shop as well as a

fashion boutique selling designer duds. The restaurant has a chef that throws together the wild tastes of both Cambodia and Taiwan. The flavors jump out at you when you first come in the place as the aromas of a dozen different spices fill the air. Favorites: Braised pork steamed bao; Grilled marinated duck hearts (I know, it sounds awful, but it's damned good); and Num Pang Sandwich with pork shoulder. Nice outdoor seating area where you can get away from the busy things going on inside the shop.

MARTIN'S TAVERN

1264 Wisconsin Ave. NW, Washington, DC, 202-333-7370;
www.martinstavern.com
CUISINE: American
DRINKS: Full Bar
SERVING: Lunch, Dinner
PRICE RANGE: $$
NEIGHBORHOOD: Georgetown
A historic family-owned tavern with mismatched Tiffany-style lamps hanging over the mahogany bar. American menu serves items like Richard M. Nixon's favorite meatloaf and President Truman's preferred pot roast.

MATCHBOX

521 8th Street, SE, Washington, DC, 202-548-0369
www.matchboxrestaurants.com
CUISINE: Pizza, American
DRINKS: Full Bar
SERVING: Lunch, Dinner
PRICE RANGE: $$

NEIGHBORHOOD: Capitol Hill/Barracks Row
Sliders, pizza, American food
Friendly neighborhood spot with great food and great
service. Good wine and beer menu. Menu favorites
include: Fire & Smoke pizza and the sliders. Patio
seating that's dog-friendly.

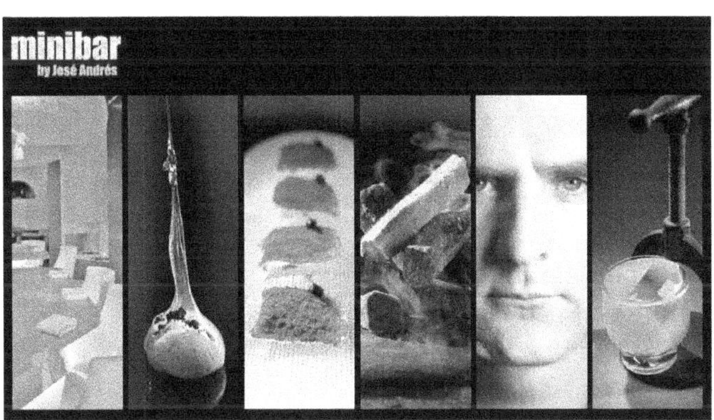

MINIBAR
855 E St. NW, Washington DC: 202-393-0812
www.minibarbyjoseandres.com
CUISINE: American
DRINKS: Full bar
SERVING: Dinner
PRICE RANGE: $$$$
Ranked #1 by Washington City Paper's list of most
powerful restaurants. An imaginative menu in an
intimate setting. Don't miss out on this dining
experience.

NOOSHI
524 8th St SE, Washington, DC, 202-827-8832
www.nooshidc.com

CUISINE: American, Sushi
DRINKS: Full Bar
SERVING: Lunch, Dinner
PRICE RANGE: $$
NEIGHBORHOOD: Capitol Hill/Barracks Row
Newly opened eatery with impressive Asian Fusion menu. Great food and friendly service. Menu favorites include: noodle Bowl with the Pork Loin, Drunken noodles, and general tao chicken.

OBELISK

2029 P St NW, Washington DC: 202-872-1180
www.obeliskdc.com
CUISINE: Italian
DRINKS: Full bar
SERVING: Dinner
PRICE RANGE: $$$$
One of the best dining experiences in DC. Delicious food and friendly service. Obelisk is a dining pleasure! Unique and inventive menu. Impressive wine selections.

OLD EBBITT GRILL

675 15th St NW, Washington, DC, 202-347-4800
www.ebbitt.com
CUISINE: American
DRINKS: Full Bar
SERVING: Breakfast, Lunch, Dinner
PRICE RANGE: $$
NEIGHBORHOOD: McPherson Square
This beautiful restaurant is a historic DC landmark. Good food and excellent service. I seldom come to DC without grabbing a seat at the bar and slurping down 2 or 3 dozen ice cold oysters. Menu favorites include: Crispy shrimp tacos, Seared Atlantic Salmon and Trout Parmesan.

OYAMEL COCINA MEXICANA

401 7th St NW, Washington, DC, 202-628-1005
www.oyamel.com
CUISINE: Mexican/Tapas Bar
DRINKS: Full bar
SERVING: Lunch & Dinner
PRICE RANGE: $$$
NEIGHBORHOOD: Penn Quarter
Upscale Mexican (not Tex-Mex) eatery offering a menu of creative Mexican fare and street food, but always with a more sophisticated approach than a street vendor would bring to the task. Tacos have Yucatan-style BBQ pork, Mexican sour orange and pickled red onion, for instance. Or try the mushroom sautéed with cream sauce and served with potato chips. Nice selection of cocktails and wine. Food served in small plates – ceviches and tacos.

PEARL DIVE OYSTER PALACE

1612 14th St. N.W., Washington, DC, 202-986-8787
www.pearldivedc.com
CUISINE: Seafood
DRINKS: Full Bar
SERVING: Dinner, Brunch
PRICE RANGE: $$$

NEIGHBORHOOD: Logan Circle
This very popular local hangout with its beat-up
furniture, a floor that could use a little varnish and the
big window overlooking the street, serves great
seafood and some of the freshest oysters in town. (If
I'm not at the Old Ebbitt Grill swallowing oysters, I
can be found here.) If you're not into raw oysters then
try the wood-grilled oysters with garlic, red chili
butter and gremolata. Or my go-to dish: the cornmeal
crusted ousters with Andouille sausage, served with a

sweet potato hash. Late night menu. Bar on the second floor.

THE PIG
1320 14th St. NW (bet. N. Rhode Island Ave & N. N St), 202-290-2821
www.thepigdc.com/
CUISINE: New American; pork focus
DRINKS: full bar, happy hour 3-7
SERVING: lunch weekdays till 4; weekend brunch; dinner nightly.
PRICE RANGE: $$$
They have their own farm in Maryland that the vegetables served here come from. Menu is focused on pork and all the great things you can do with it. Radish & arugula salad, charred caesar (with duck egg and grilled cheese-anchovy croutons), roasted beets. Pig dish favorites: braised cheek, wild boar ragu over pappardelle, pulled pork mac n cheese, pork & lamb meatballs served over grits in a stewed tomato sauce.

PIZZA PARADISO
2003 P St. NW, Washington DC: 202-223-1245
3282 M St. NW, Washington DC: 202-337-1245
www.eatyourpizza.com
CUISINE: Pizza
DRINKS: Full bar
SERVING: Lunch, Dinner
PRICE RANGE: $$
Great pizza, friendly bartenders, and fun atmosphere. Beware of the lines and the noise level but overall very comfortable. Impressive beer selection.

THE PRIME RIB

2020 K St. NW, Washington DC: 202-466-8811
https://theprimeribs.com/
CUISINE: Steakhouse, Seafood
DRINKS: Full bar
SERVING: Lunch, Dinner
PRICE RANGE: $$$$
Zagat's #1 Rated Steakhouse in DC. The Prime Rib
features USDA Prime Dry Aged NY Strip Steaks &
USDA Filet Mignon. Casual dress at lunch, jackets
after 5 p.m. Live piano music nightly.

QUEEN'S ENGLISH

3410 11th St NW, Washington, No Phone
www.queensenglishdc.com
CUISINE: Hong Kong-style cafe
DRINKS: Full bar
SERVING: Dinner; Closed Sun & Mon

PRICE RANGE: $$$
NEIGHBORHOOD: Columbia Heights
Upscale but at the same time charming and intimate
spot offering Hong Kong cuisine on a unique and
ever-changing menu. Take a good look at the colorful
wallpaper with bursting colors that remind me motifs
in Chinese art I've seen over the years. Favorites: Soy
braised enoki mushroom; Twice cooked pork rib.
Impressive wine list.

RAPPAHANNOCK OYSTER BAR

1309 5th St. NE, Washington, DC, 202-544-4702
www.rroysters.com
CUISINE: Seafood, Bar
DRINKS: Beer and Wine only
SERVING: Lunch, Dinner
PRICE RANGE: $$
Inside the busy-as-ever Union Market is this small bar
with countertop that seats about 12. Small menu with
items like great fresh oysters, crab cakes and beer.
This place is run by one of the oldest family-operated
Chesapeake Bay oyster families, so the product they
bring in—the Olde Salts oysters and the soft
Rappahannocks variety—are all great.

RASIKA

633 D St. NW, Washington, DC: 202-637-1222
1190 New Hampshire Ave. NW, Washington DC:
202-466-2500
www.rasikarestaurant.com
CUISINE: Indian
DRINKS: Full bar
SERVING: Lunch, Dinner
PRICE RANGE: $$$
Excellent Indian restaurant with a fine dining
experience. Vegan selections. Delicious entrees like
the Papeta Ringna Nu Shak, which is potatoes and
Indian eggplant cooked with mustard seeds in a
tomato sauce and topped with cilantro. If you're a fan
of Indian food then this is the place. Make
reservations.

RISTORANTE TOSCA

1112 F St NW, Washington, DC, 202-367-1990
www.toscadc.com
CUISINE: Italian
DRINKS: Full bar
SERVING: Lunch & Dinner; Dinner only on Sat;
closed Sun – dress nicely.
PRICE RANGE: $$$
NEIGHBORHOOD: Downtown
Upscale dining featuring waiters in formal uniforms
serving from a menu of fine Northern Italian fare.
Definitely a place for serious grownups, no kids. Half
the bills that actually get through Congress are
probably discussed here first, by lobbyists paying for

every meal. You're first impressed by the "beigeness" of the room—muted colors of saddle, khaki, camel, ecru, biscuit, tan, cream—you get the idea. Nothing too jolting. Don't raise your voice. By all means choose the pasta here—it's sublime. Menu favorites include: Lobster ravioli and Bucatini. Very attentive service. Crunchy bread, good coffee from a French press. Great wine list.

ROOSTER & OWL
2436 14th St NW, Washington, 202-813-3976
www.roosterowl.com
CUISINE: American (New)
DRINKS: Full bar
SERVING: Dinner; Closed Sun & Mon
PRICE RANGE: $$$
NEIGHBORHOOD: Columbia Heights
Popular eatery featuring market-driven New American cuisine. Big emphasis on fresh vegetables, and they prepare everything expertly. Has an

affordable pre-fixe menu that I usually select when I'm here. Sharing plates also popular. Fun place with a good vibe. You get that, "I'm glad I chose this place" feeling when you sit down. Favorites: Short Rib and Maryland crab cake. Wine pairings available.

ROSE'S LUXURY
717 8th St SE, Washington, DC, 202-580-8889
www.rosesluxury.com
CUISINE: American (New)/Pastas
DRINKS: Full bar
SERVING: Dinner; closed Sun
PRICE RANGE: $$$
NEIGHBORHOOD: Capital Hill
Located in a converted townhouse, this eatery features a creative menu of New American tapas and an upstairs lounge. If you don't want to wait for a table, you can eat at the kitchen counter facing the open kitchen. Menu changes often but some of the popular dishes include: Pork & lychee salad and Grilled Veal. Arrive early as this place gets packed. Reservations recommended.

RUSSIA HOUSE
1800 Connecticut Ave NW, Washington, DC, 202-234-9433
www.russiahouselounge.com
CUISINE: Russian
DRINKS: Full Bar
SERVING: Dinner
PRICE RANGE: $$$
NEIGHBORHOOD: Dupont Circle
This restaurant/lounge lives up to its name with its extensive list of vodkas. Try the sampler which lets you select any 5 vodkas to taste. Nice menu. Favorites include: Potato Mushroom Cocotte, Chicken Kiev, and Vareniki and Cauliflower. Excellent service.

SEVEN REASONS
2208 14th St NW, Washington, 202-417-8563
www.sevenreasonsdc.com

CUISINE: Latin American
DRINKS: Full bar
SERVING: Dinner; Closed on Mondays
PRICE RANGE: $$$
NEIGHBORHOOD: NorthWest
Old brick walls give a warm feeling in this multi-level eatery that offers a unique culinary experience with a great interior décor. These Latin-inspired dishes are meant to be shared. Prepared by a Venezuelan chef, he brings all the influences of Venezuela (Spanish, Italian, Indian, Chinese) that are reflected in the highly diverse cuisine of that country. The chef (like most Uber drivers I have in Miami) fled Venezuela's political & social turmoil for a better place—and he ended up here in DC where he's got this truly fabulous restaurant. Visit him. You'll love it as much as I did. Favorites: Lamb loin palo-a-pique; Swordfish belly and trout roe; and Royal sea bass ceviche.

SWEETGREEN
1512 Connecticut Ave. NW, Washington DC, 202-387-9338
www.sweetgreen.com
CUISINE: Ice Cream & Frozen Yogurt, Fruits & Veggies
DRINKS: No Booze
SERVING: Lunch
PRICE RANGE: $$
NEIGHBORHOOD: Dupont Circle
Salad bar with a unique selection of locally sourced vegetables mixed into combinations like spicy sabzi, a mixture of baby spinach, roasted broccoli, quinoa, a

squirt of sriracha and chile-carrot vinaigrette.
Interesting selection of healthy beverages.

TED'S BULLETIN
505 8th St SE, Washington, DC, 202-544-8337
www.tedsbulletin.com
CUISINE: American
DRINKS: Full Bar
SERVING: Breakfast, Lunch, Dinner
PRICE RANGE: $$
NEIGHBORHOOD: Capitol Hill/Barracks Row
A popular spot with a retro-diner feel serving
American favorites like tomato soup and grilled
cheese sandwiches. Speaking of retro, the homemade
twinkies and pop-tarts. Great milkshakes. They also
have "cocktail" milkshakes, like the Dirty Girl Scout,
tarted up with peppermint schnapps.

THIP KHAO

3462 14th St NW, Washington, 202-387-5426
www.thipkhao.com
CUISINE: Laotian
DRINKS: Full bar
SERVING: Lunch, Dinner
PRICE RANGE: $$
NEIGHBORHOOD: Columbia Heights
Modern eatery offering genuine Laotian cuisine.
Nothing particularly intriguing about the interior here.
What brought me here was the food, because it's very
difficult to get genuine Laotian cuisine prepared by
somebody who knows what they're doing. What
you'll find here is the real thing. Special fish and pork
dishes, some of which have red hot spices that will
burn your tongue off. (Stay away from the Red Goat
Curry! I'm sure I'd have like it if I could've tasted it,
LOL.) Super inventive salad bursting with fresh and
different flavor combinations. Favorites: Khao siin;

Crispy coconut-rice salad with fermented pork (nam khao). Classic cocktails.

TOKI UNDERGROUND
1234 H St NE, Washington, DC, 202-388-3086
www.tokiunderground.com
CUISINE: Asian Fusion
DRINKS: Full Bar
SERVING: Dinner
PRICE RANGE: $$
NEIGHBORHOOD: H Street Corridor/Atlas District/Near Northeast
A trendy Taiwanese-style ramen bar decorated with skateboards and featuring punk/indie music. Authentic ramen dishes such as pulled pork, egg, vegetables and broth. Cocktails and good selection of Japanese beer. Excellent staff.

TRIO RESTAURANT
1537 17th St. NW, Washington, DC: 202-232-6305
www.triodc.com
CUISINE: American
DRINKS: Full bar
SERVING: Lunch, Dinner, Brunch
PRICE RANGE: $$
Neighborhood diner with outdoor seating. Typical diner food but specials shine. Good friendly service. A favorite of locals so you know it's good. Best bets are the Trio sliders, wild mushroom ravioli, and fish Spanish style. Burgers are also a good choice.

THE UGLY MUG

723 8th Street, SE, Washington, DC, 202-547-8459
www.uglymugdc.com
CUISINE: American
DRINKS: Full Bar
SERVING: Lunch, Dinner, Late Night
PRICE RANGE: $$
NEIGHBORHOOD: Capitol Hill/Barracks Row
Sports bar with great menu, has the feel of a college
bar. Menu favorites: Sliders and Buffalo Chicken.
Friendly staff.

UNION MARKET

1309 5th St NE, Washington, DC, 301-347-3998
www.unionmarketdc.com
Union Market is an artisanal food market with over
40 local vendors from up and coming to established
restaurateurs. Some of the venues include:
Rappahannock Oyster Co., Buffalo & Bergen,
Righteous Cheese, Peregrine Espresso, Lyon Bakery,

Trickling Springs Creamery, Harvey's Market, Oh! Pickles, Almaala Farms, DC Empanadas and TaKorean. Wonderful place to spend half a day. (Or even a full day.)

ZAYTINYA
701 9th St. NW, Washington, DC: 202-638-0800
www.zaytinya.com
CUISINE: Turkish, Greek,
DRINKS: Full bar
SERVING: Lunch, Dinner
PRICE RANGE: $$$
Great place to take out-of-town guests. Beautiful interior with two-level dining area. Menu favorites include: Labneh, Tzatziki, Htipiti, Tabouleh, Kolokithokeftedes (zucchini fritters), Seared

Halloumi Cheese, Mushroom Couscous, Patates Tiganites Me Yiaourti (French fries) and Havuç Köftesi (carrot apricot fritters). Great vegetarian selections.

NIGHTLIFE

U Street is a happening place for nightlife in Washington. Adams Morgan used to be the busiest, but now there's lot of activity on U.

THE BRIXTON

901 U St NW, Washington, DC, 202-525-4834
www.brixtondc.com
NEIGHBORHOOD: U Street
Trendy multi-level hangout – first floor British pub, second floor lounge and roof deck with two bars. It all feels very much like a British country hunting lodge with deer antler chandeliers, old black-and-white pictures from the past. This place attracts a crowd of regulars. Bar menu of snacks like sliders, calamari and burgers.

CHURCHKEY

1337 14th St NW, Washington, DC, 202-567-2576.
www.churchkeydc.com
NEIGHBORHOOD: Logan Circle
Located near the galleries on 14th Street, this place has an unbelievable beer selection with 50 on draft and over 500 in bottles. Bar menu with items like mac n cheese and the brat burger.

H STREET COUNTRY CLUB

1335 H St NE, Washington, DC, 202-399-4722
www.thehstreetcountryclub.com
NEIGHBORHOOD: H Street Corridor
Essentially this is a bar with lots of games including
miniature golf. Multiple bars, rooftop patio. Drink
specials.

THE GIBSON

2009 14th St. NW, Washington: 202-629-1081
thegibsondc.com/
They offer experienced mixologists here, so come for
the swanky cocktail creations. Perfect place for a

romantic get together: dark, lots of candles, appropriate music. Only holds 50 people at the bar and at a few tables. Because it's popular and they do not allow you to stand around the way they do in other bars, you have to reserve to get in on busy nights. If you show up without a reservation, you give your cell # to the doorman who will call you when space opens up. Unusual, huh? While you wait, you can drift off to nearby watering holes to explore. (Not usually a wait Sunday-Thursday.)

MARTIN'S TAVERN
1264 Wisconsin Ave. NW, Washington, DC, 202-333-7370;
www.martinstavern.com
WEBSITE DOWN AT PRESSTIME
NEIGHBORHOOD: Georgetown

A historic family-owned tavern with mismatched Tiffany-style lamps hanging over the mahogany bar. American menu serves items like Richard M. Nixon's favorite meatloaf and President Truman's preferred pot roast.

OFF THE RECORD AT THE HAY-ADAMS
800 16th St NW, Washington, DC, 202-638-6600
www.hayadams.com
NEIGHBORHOOD: Downtown

Elegant old bar with wooden furniture and ornate walls covered with pictures, drawings and charicatures of politicians, current and past, with colorful interpretations of the subjects. Bar serves classic coctails (like Manhattans and Old Fashioneds) any pol would love. Nice bar menu.

ROUND ROBIN BAR
WILLARD HOTEL
1401 Pennsylvania Ave NW, Washington, 202-637-7348
https://washington.intercontinental.com
NEIGHBORHOOD: Penn Quarter
Located in the luxury Willard Hotel, this upscale, century-old lounge serves classic cocktails. Old school ambiance. Nice menu of bar nibbles. Legend has it that Ulysses S. Grant coining the term "lobbyists" as a label for those who chased after him

in the Willard's lobby beseeching him for jobs in his Administration. (Ask the bartender about the artist who drew the illustrations on the walls—very interesting story.)

ST REGIS BAR
The St. Regis
923 16th St NW, Washington, 202-638-2626
www.stregiswashingtondc.com
NEIGHBORHOOD: Downtown
Located inside the St. Regis Hotel, this beautifully decorated lounge serves up handcrafted cocktails and a menu of upscale bar snacks. This classic bar is an ideal stop for cocktails, light bites and conversation, not to mention people watching if you're into high rollers and DC power types.

THE TOMBS
1226 36th St. NW, Washington, DC, 202-337-6668
www.tombs.com
NEIGHBORHOOD: Georgetown
Since 1962, The Tombs has been a popular gathering place for Georgetown students. TVs for watching the game. Also popular spot for Sunday brunch.

INDEX

<table>
<tr><td>

A

</td><td>

B

</td></tr>
</table>

U

V

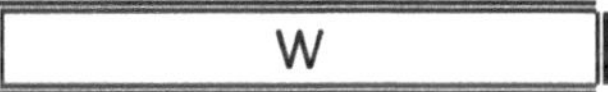
W

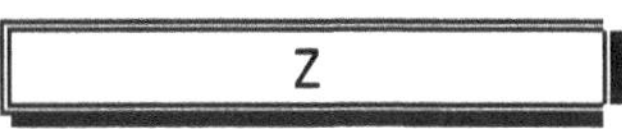
Z